Big Data Analytics

Nitin Kumar Yadav

Published by NotesKaro Inc, 2025.

BIG DATA ANALYTICS

First edition. May 25, 2025.

ISBN: 979-8231037247

Written by Nitin Kumar Yadav.

Table of Contents

Dedication

I dedicate this book to each curious mind, each self-learner, and every character who dares to study beyond limitations—past the fear of complexity, past the strain of checks, and beyond the partitions of classrooms. This book is for you—the reader who desires to understand, not simply memorize... who wants to learn something real, some thing treasured, something destiny-prepared.

the adventure of writing this e-book did no longer start in a formal putting or below instructional pressure. It commenced from a want I noticed in students, rookies, and specialists around me—suffering with bulky textbooks, complicated language, and scattered assets. I regularly saw those who truely desired to apprehend technologies like massive statistics and Hadoop, but gave up sincerely because the to be had cloth become either too technical, too advanced, or too tough to relate with. That truth stayed with me.

As a person who enjoys both generation and creativity, I usually believed that getting to know ought to no longer sense like a burden—it have to feel like discovery. I wanted to create some thing that simplifies matters without losing their essence, something that explains why as well as how, and something that connects with the learner in simple, human language.

This e book is born out of that concept:

To create a aid that speaks to the learner without delay.

To make big information and Hadoop—a topic regularly feared—into something anyone can approach, apprehend, and use.

I didn't need to jot down just another educational book full of definitions, diagrams, and ritual. I wanted to jot down something that appears like a conversation—wherein the reader feels guided, not overloaded. I desired to write in a language that's close to the way we assume and talk, no longer in jargon that pushes human beings away. for my part, readability is greater powerful than complexity, and ease is a kind of intelligence.

So I determined to write the whole lot from scratch.

No reproduction-paste. No shortcuts. No fillers.

each sentence on this book is unique, written with the intention that someone who's analyzing it could virtually experience, "sure, i am getting this now."

for the duration of this ebook, you'll discover explanations in place of assumptions. Examples as opposed to empty principle. And mainly, you'll find a regular tone that announces—you're capable, and that is for you.

This dedication is also for the ones newbies who might not have get entry to to high priced coaching, fancy tutorials, or formal college steering. I recognize how hard it is able to be to have a look at while your environment is not supportive, or while the internet floods you with content material however gives you no direction. i hope this e-book brings some shape, readability, and confidence into your getting to know adventure.

penning this ebook additionally gave me a danger to mirror on the bigger role that information performs in shaping our international. we are living in an technology in which records is power, and getting to know the way to manage and examine that statistics can open limitless doorways. whether or not you're a scholar, a running expert, or a person simply exploring tech out of curiosity, knowledge big records and tools like Hadoop can absolutely remodel the way you look at facts.

I dedicate this work to the concept that education have to no longer be a privilege—it should be a opportunity for all of us. nobody ought to be saved away from know-how simply due to the fact the books are too tough to examine, the language is too technical, or the cloth is scattered and difficult. That's why I focused now not just on what to write, however a way to write it, so that every person picking this book can stroll away feeling enlightened, no longer crushed.

To all the ones who have ever felt like giving up on a subject due to the fact they couldn't discover the right book—this is for you.

To all people who are beginning from scratch and sense lost—that is for you.

To all individuals who want to move in advance in lifestyles through mastering something meaningful—that is for you.

This e-book is likewise a small however sincere try and give back to the network—the learners, the readers, the silent fighters of understanding. I may not know your name or your story, however I recognise this: you deserve content that respects your time, intelligence, and effort.

If this book could make even one hard idea feel less complicated...

If it could assist even one student advantage self belief...

If it could inspire even one learner to maintain going...

Then the infinite hours of studies, writing, modifying, and rewriting behind this e-book might be without a doubt well worth it.

– Nitin Kumar Yadav

Board of directors, Sellbrochure IPDP

writer, creator, and Believer in easy, powerful learninglearning

We stay in an age in which data has emerge as the new oil—a limiteless resource that drives selections, innovations, and revolutions across industries. From e-trade and healthcare to finance, governance, and social media, facts is being generated at an exponential price. each click, swipe, sensor reading, transaction, and interaction produces massive volumes of digital information, frequently in real time. This explosion of records has given birth to a new domain—huge facts—which no longer only captures the essence of records boom but also the assignment of extracting cost from it.

inside the past, information changed into regularly saved in established codecs like tables or spreadsheets. today, however, the virtual universe includes text, images, movies, logs, sensor statistics, internet information, and unstructured social content material. these styles of records exceed the capacity of conventional tools, both in scale and complexity. this is where massive records technology, led by using Apache Hadoop, play a important role.

Hadoop emerged no longer just as a tool but as a paradigm shift—from storing and analyzing records in a single vicinity to distributing it throughout clusters of machines, enabling parallel processing of petabytes of information with fault tolerance and scalability. at the heart of Hadoop lies the Hadoop dispensed document gadget (HDFS), which breaks records into blocks and distributes them across nodes for green storage and retrieval. alongside it, MapReduce gives a programming version that simplifies the process of writing allotted applications.

however Hadoop is more than simply HDFS and MapReduce. it is a whole environment built to deal with numerous duties within the massive statistics pipeline. gear like Pig and Hive allow high-stage querying and data manipulation. HBase gives NoSQL skills, even as Sqoop and Flume permit smooth ingestion of facts from various resources. Oozie, Zookeeper, and Mahout bring scheduling, coordination, and machine mastering into the combination. This environment transforms Hadoop right into a whole platform—one that not handiest shops statistics however also analyzes, learns, and acts.

This e book is a gateway into that environment.

The purpose of this e-book isn't always most effective to educate Hadoop but also to offer readers with an intuitive information of how big records structures function in real-life scenarios. Written in easy English and enriched with clean examples, the e-book takes you from the basics of virtual records types to the architectural concepts of Hadoop and in the end into implemented analytics with R and gadget gaining knowledge of.

chapter with the aid of chapter, the reader will find out how the history of Hadoop started with Google's pioneering paintings on the Google document gadget and MapReduce model, which stimulated the open-supply Hadoop framework. From there, we discover HDFS extensive, know-how the way it offers fault tolerance, scalability, and excessive throughput for huge-scale statistics processing. Readers are delivered to command-line interfaces, records flows, ingestion tools like Flume and Sqoop, and vital garage practices the usage of Hadoop information.

within the chapters on MapReduce, we ruin down the anatomy of a task run—inspecting mission execution, failure healing, shuffle and sort mechanisms, and special activity codecs. those insights help readers build a stable understanding of distributed computing logic and optimization strategies utilized in actual-international structures.

The Hadoop atmosphere is then explored through actual equipment and structures. With Pig, readers research scripting-based records manipulation the usage of Pig Latin. In Hive, square-like querying becomes the bridge between traditional relational databases and contemporary huge information structures. HBase introduces NoSQL ideas, making it less difficult to address dynamic and sparse data. The section on massive sq. offers readers a glimpse into how traditional sq. can scale to meet the needs of large facts analytics.

The very last unit introduces information Analytics with R—a language celebrated for its statistical abilities and graphing strength. by using the use of R, analysts can visualize traits, discover relationships, and construct statistical and system mastering models. The e-book in addition explores supervised mastering strategies like type and regression, in addition to unsupervised gaining knowledge of strategies like clustering. It even touches upon collaborative filtering, which forms the spine of current advice structures.

beyond tools and technology, this e book additionally emphasizes the philosophy of information. It explores how records, while processed efficaciously, can cause insightful decisions, strategic changes, and social effect.

UNIT I: INTRODUCTION TO BIG DATA AND HADOOP

TYPES OF DIGITAL DATA

Digital data is information that is stored in binary form and can be processed by computers. It comes in different types:

1. Structured Data – This data follows a fixed format, like rows and columns in databases (e.g., MySQL tables).

2. SEMI-STRUCTURED Data – This data doesn't follow a strict format but still contains tags or markers to separate elements (e.g., XML, JSON).

3. UNSTRUCTURED DATA – This includes data without a predefined model, such as images, videos, emails, social media content, etc.

Introduction to Big Data

Big Data refers to extremely large datasets that cannot be handled efficiently using traditional data processing tools. It is characterized by the 5 V's:

Volume – Huge amount of data.

Velocity – Fast generation and processing of data.

Variety – Different types of data (text, audio, video).

Veracity – Uncertainty in data accuracy.

Value – Meaningful insights that can be extracted from data.

BIG DATA REQUIRES ADVANCED tools and technologies to store, manage, and analyze efficiently.

Big Data Analytics

Big Data Analytics is the process of examining large datasets to uncover hidden patterns, correlations, and insights. It helps organizations in decision-making, predicting trends, and improving services. Tools like Hadoop, Spark, and R are commonly used for Big Data Analytics.

History of Hadoop

Hadoop started as a project by Doug Cutting and Mike Cafarella inspired by Google's File System (GFS). It was later adopted by Yahoo and became an open-source Apache project. Hadoop was designed to store and process big data across clusters of computers using simple programming models.

APACHE HADOOP

Apache Hadoop is an open-source framework that allows for distributed processing of large datasets across many computers using a simple programming model. It consists of:

HDFS (Hadoop Distributed File System) – For storage.

MapReduce – For processing.

YARN – For resource management.

Common Utilities – Shared tools and libraries.

Analyzing Data with Unix Tools

Before Hadoop, simple Unix tools like grep, awk, sort, and sed were used for analyzing log files and textual data. These tools are fast for small datasets but not scalable for big data due to memory and processing limits.

ANALYZING DATA WITH Hadoop

Hadoop enables analysis of large data sets in a distributed manner. It breaks down large data into smaller chunks, stores them in HDFS, and processes them in parallel using MapReduce. This allows faster and efficient data analysis compared to traditional methods.

Hadoop Streaming

Hadoop Streaming is a utility that allows users to create and run MapReduce jobs with any executable or script as the mapper and/or reducer. It supports languages like Python, Perl, or even shell scripts. This makes it flexible for developers who are not familiar with Java.

Hadoop Ecosystem

The Hadoop ecosystem is a collection of tools and services built around Hadoop to perform various data processing tasks. Key components include:

Pig – High-level data flow language.

Hive – SQL-like query engine for Hadoop.

HBase – NoSQL database.

Sqoop – Data transfer between Hadoop and relational databases.

Flume – Ingesting log and event data.

Zookeeper – Coordination service.

Oozie – Workflow scheduler.

IBM Big Data Strategy

IBM focuses on using Big Data to generate insights and drive innovation. Their strategy includes:

Providing scalable platforms like IBM InfoSphere BigInsights.

Offering tools for real-time analytics.

Integrating Hadoop with enterprise systems.

Ensuring security and governance for big data.

Introduction to InfoSphere BigInsights and BigSheets

IBM InfoSphere BigInsights is IBM's Big Data platform built on Apache Hadoop. It provides enterprise-grade features like analytics, visualization, and security.

BigSheets is a web-based spreadsheet tool included in BigInsights that allows non-programmers to analyze big data using a familiar Excel-like interface.

Great! Here's a more detailed version of UNIT II in easy English, written originally for your textbook publication. The content is structured in paragraph form, with minimal points, and fully explained for clarity.

UNIT II: HDFS (Hadoop Distributed File System)

THE DESIGN OF HDFS

HDFS stands for Hadoop Distributed File System, which is a core part of the Hadoop framework. It is specially designed to store very large files across a network of machines in a distributed manner. The goal of HDFS is to provide reliable, fault-tolerant, and high-throughput access to data.

HDFS follows a master-slave architecture. The master is called the NameNode, and the slaves are called DataNodes. The NameNode is responsible for managing the file system namespace, such as keeping track of the files, directories, and metadata (information about data like file permissions, size, and location). The actual data is stored in the DataNodes in the form of blocks. By default, each file is broken into 128MB blocks and stored across different DataNodes. These blocks are also replicated (default replication factor is 3) to handle failures and ensure data reliability. If one node fails, the same data can be accessed from its replica.

HDFS Concepts

Several key concepts form the foundation of HDFS:

Blocks: Files are split into blocks (usually 128 MB or 256 MB) and stored separately.

Replication: Each block is stored in multiple nodes (default is 3 copies) to ensure fault tolerance.

Write-once, read-many: HDFS is optimized for applications where files are written once and read many times.

High throughput: HDFS is built for high data transfer rates rather than low latency.

Fault Tolerance: It can recover from DataNode failures automatically using replicas.

Command Line Interface (CLI)

HDFS provides a powerful command-line interface that allows users to interact with the file system using shell commands. Some basic commands include:

hdfs dfs -ls / – List the contents of a directory

hdfs dfs -put localfile /hdfs/path/ – Upload a file from the local system to HDFS

hdfs dfs -get /hdfs/file localdir/ – Download a file from HDFS to the local file system

hdfs dfs -rm /file – Delete a file from HDFS

THESE COMMANDS HELP users perform day-to-day operations such as copying files, checking file status, and managing the HDFS file system.

Hadoop File System Interfaces

Hadoop offers various interfaces to interact with HDFS:

1. Command Line Interface (CLI) – As discussed above, it allows direct file operations.

---

2. JAVA API – DEVELOPERS can write Java programs to read/write data into HDFS using FileSystem class.

---

3. HDFS WEB UI – A browser-based user interface that displays information about NameNode, DataNodes, storage usage, etc.

---

4. BROWSER-BASED FILE Access – HDFS files can also be accessed via REST APIs (like WebHDFS).

---

5. FS SHELL – IT PROVIDES shell-like commands for file operations similar to Unix.

Data Flow in HDFS

THE DATA FLOW IN HDFS describes how data is written and read. When a user uploads a file:

The client first communicates with the NameNode to get the location of available DataNodes.

The file is split into blocks, and the client sends each block to the designated DataNodes.

The block is stored in the first DataNode, which then forwards it to the second, and then the third (this is called pipeline replication).

The NameNode keeps metadata about where each block of the file is stored.

WHEN READING A FILE, the client again contacts the NameNode to get the list of DataNodes holding the blocks and then retrieves the blocks directly from the DataNodes.

Data Ingest with Flume and Sqoop

Getting data into Hadoop is known as data ingestion. Hadoop supports two popular tools for this:

Flume: Flume is used to collect, aggregate, and move large volumes of log data from various sources like web servers into HDFS. It is reliable and can handle streaming data in real-time. It uses agents that define source, channel, and sink to transport the data.

Sqoop: Sqoop (SQL-to-Hadoop) is used for importing and exporting data between Hadoop and relational databases like MySQL, Oracle, and SQL Server. It can import tables from RDBMS into HDFS as text files or Avro formats and can also export processed data back into relational databases.

Hadoop Archives (HAR)

Hadoop Archives (HAR) are used to manage a large number of small files in HDFS. Normally, HDFS works best with large files. When there are too many small files, it creates problems for the NameNode, which stores metadata. HAR combines many small files into a single file structure, reducing the load on the NameNode. Although HAR helps in space optimization, reading performance may be slightly reduced.

Hadoop I/O: Compression, Serialization, Avro, and File-Based Data Structures

Compression: Hadoop supports compression to save storage space and improve performance. Compressed files reduce the amount of data transferred between HDFS and MapReduce. Some common compression formats are Gzip, Bzip2, Snappy, and LZO. Compression can be used at input, intermediate, and output stages.

Serialization: Serialization is the process of converting objects into a byte stream for storage or transmission. Hadoop uses Writable classes for serialization. Custom data types must implement the Writable and WritableComparable interfaces to work with Hadoop jobs.

AVRO: AVRO IS A ROW-based serialization framework developed within the Hadoop ecosystem. It supports schema evolution, which means you can change the structure of data without breaking the existing processing. Avro files are compact, fast, and suitable for interchanging data between different languages and systems.

File-Based Data Structures: Hadoop supports different file formats to store and process data efficiently:

Text Files: Simple and human-readable but not optimized for large-scale processing.

Sequence Files: Binary files that store data as key-value pairs. Used within MapReduce.

Avro Files: Compact and suitable for long-term data storage.

Parquet/ORC: Columnar storage formats optimized for queries (mostly used with Hive and Spark).

UNIT III: MapReduce

INTRODUCTION TO MAPREDUCE

MapReduce is a programming model and processing technique used in Hadoop to process large volumes of data in a distributed and parallel manner. It simplifies data processing by dividing a task into two major phases: Map and Reduce. The Map phase processes input data and produces intermediate key-value pairs. The Reduce phase takes these intermediate pairs, combines them, and produces the final output.

The advantage of MapReduce is that it allows processing to be done across many machines in parallel, which improves performance and scalability. This model is ideal for problems that require analysis of massive datasets, such as counting words, summarizing logs, or analyzing customer behavior.

Anatomy of a MapReduce Job Run

When a MapReduce program is executed in Hadoop, several steps are followed:

1. Input Splits: The input file is divided into chunks called input splits (usually 128MB each). Each split is processed by a separate mapper.

---

2. MAP PHASE: MAPPERS read the split data and produce intermediate key-value pairs.

---

3. SHUFFLE AND SORT: The intermediate data is transferred across the network to the reducers. During this phase, the data is grouped by keys and sorted.

---

4. REDUCE PHASE: REDUCERS aggregate the grouped data and produce the final output.

---

5. OUTPUT: THE FINAL result is written back to HDFS.

The JobTracker (in Hadoop 1.x) or ResourceManager (in Hadoop 2.x/YARN) manages the overall execution, including task assignment, resource monitoring, and fault handling.

FAILURES IN MAPREDUCE

MapReduce is designed to handle failures automatically:

If a Mapper or Reducer fails, the job tracker or resource manager will restart the failed task on another node.

If a DataNode fails, Hadoop can still read the data from its replicas stored on other nodes.

The system keeps track of progress and logs errors, making it easy to identify failed jobs or tasks.

BECAUSE OF THIS, MAPREDUCE ensures fault tolerance and data reliability without user intervention.

Job Scheduling

Job scheduling in MapReduce decides which jobs run at what time and on which nodes. Hadoop uses a scheduler to assign available resources to jobs.

Common types of schedulers include:

FIFO (First In First Out): Jobs are executed in the order they arrive.

Fair Scheduler: Resources are divided fairly between all jobs.

Capacity Scheduler: Resources are divided into queues with limits, allowing multiple users or departments to share the cluster efficiently.

SCHEDULING ENSURES efficient use of resources, especially in a shared environment.

Shuffle and Sort

The shuffle and sort phase occurs between the map and reduce phases. It is a critical step in the MapReduce process:

Shuffle: This involves transferring intermediate key-value pairs from the mappers to the appropriate reducers based on keys.

Sort: The data is sorted by key before being passed to the reducer. Hadoop automatically performs sorting so that reducers can process data in order.

THIS PHASE INVOLVES network I/O, and optimizing shuffle and sort is important for job performance.

Task Execution

Each map and reduce task is executed in a task container managed by YARN (Yet Another Resource Negotiator). These containers run in parallel across the Hadoop cluster. Task execution includes setting up the environment, executing the user's code, writing logs, and cleaning up resources after completion.

Hadoop monitors each task and restarts it if it fails. Each task also reports progress to the resource manager or application master, which helps detect slow or failed nodes.

MapReduce Types and Formats

MapReduce supports different input and output formats:

TextInputFormat: Reads lines of text files; each line becomes a record.

KeyValueTextInputFormat: Splits each line into key and value based on a delimiter.

SequenceFileInputFormat: Reads binary key-value pairs from sequence files.

DBInputFormat: Reads records from relational databases.

OUTPUT FORMATS CAN also vary, such as TextOutputFormat, SequenceFileOutputFormat, or custom formats defined by the developer. These formats allow flexibility depending on data type and target storage.

MapReduce Features

Some key features of MapReduce include:

Scalability: Can process petabytes of data across thousands of machines.

Fault Tolerance: Automatically handles hardware and task failures.

Parallelism: Tasks run in parallel for faster performance.

Simplicity: Developers can write simple Java programs using map and reduce methods.

Integration: MapReduce integrates well with tools like Hive, Pig, and HBase.

Customizability: Developers can define their own partitioners, comparators, and input/output formats.

UNIT IV: Hadoop Ecosystem

THE HADOOP ECOSYSTEM is not just limited to HDFS and MapReduce. It includes several powerful tools that help in data analysis, processing, querying, and storage. Popular tools like Pig, Hive, HBase, and Big SQL make working with large datasets easier and more flexible.

INTRODUCTION TO PIG

Apache Pig is a high-level platform for processing large data sets. It uses a language called Pig Latin, which is similar to SQL but designed for large-scale data manipulation. Pig allows developers to write complex data analysis tasks using fewer lines of code than Java MapReduce.

Pig is especially useful for data transformation, filtering, joining, and aggregation. It handles both structured and semi-structured data and is often used in data cleansing and ETL (Extract, Transform, Load) processes.

Execution Modes of Pig

Pig can be executed in two main modes:

1. Local Mode: Runs on a single machine and is used for small datasets or testing.

---

2. MAPREDUCE MODE: Runs on a Hadoop cluster and is used for large datasets. Pig scripts are converted into MapReduce jobs automatically.

Comparison of Pig with Databases

Pig is not a database system but a data processing tool. While SQL queries in databases work on structured data in tables, Pig works on data from HDFS and is better suited for unstructured or semi-structured data. Pig supports nested data structures and is more flexible for complex transformations.

Grunt Shell

The Grunt shell is an interactive shell provided by Pig where users can type Pig Latin commands directly and see results. It is useful for testing scripts or working step-by-step on a dataset.

Pig Latin

Pig Latin is a data flow language that uses commands like LOAD, FILTER, JOIN, GROUP, and FOREACH to process data. For example:

A = LOAD 'data.txt' AS (name, age);

B = FILTER A BY age > 25;

This script loads a file and filters records where age is more than 25.

User Defined Functions (UDFs)

Pig allows users to write their own functions in languages like Java, Python, or JavaScript to perform special tasks. These are called UDFs and help extend Pig's capabilities.

Data Processing Operators

Pig provides several built-in operators to transform data:

FILTER to remove unwanted rows

FOREACH to apply transformations

JOIN to combine datasets

GROUP and COGROUP to group data These operators make it easy to build complex workflows for big data.

Hive Shell

Hive is a data warehouse tool built on top of Hadoop. It allows users to query and manage large datasets using a language called HiveQL, which is similar to SQL. The Hive Shell is the command-line interface used to run HiveQL commands and interact with data stored in HDFS.

Hive Services

Hive provides various services:

CLI (Command Line Interface)

Web UI for graphical interface

HiveServer2 for connecting applications like Tableau or JDBC tools

Metastore, which stores metadata like table schemas and partitions

Hive Metastore

The Metastore is a critical component of Hive. It stores information about tables, columns, partitions, and data types. This metadata helps Hive understand how to read and write data from HDFS.

Comparison with Traditional Databases

Hive is similar to traditional databases in query language but differs in purpose:

Hive is not suitable for real-time processing.

It is optimized for batch processing and big data analytics.

Unlike relational databases, Hive queries are converted to MapReduce jobs in the background.

HiveQL

HiveQL is a SQL-like language used in Hive. It supports operations like:

SELECT, WHERE, GROUP BY, ORDER BY

JOIN, UNION, and INSERT INTO Example:

SELECT NAME, SALARY FROM employees WHERE salary > 50000;

This will return employees with salaries above 50,000 from HDFS tables.

Tables in Hive

Hive supports two types of tables:

Managed Tables: Hive manages both data and metadata.

External Tables: Hive manages only metadata; data remains outside Hive's control.

Querying Data

Once a table is created and loaded with data, Hive can perform queries to analyze and summarize large datasets. Users can also perform joins and aggregations similar to SQL.

User Defined Functions (UDFs)

Hive supports UDFs to perform custom operations in HiveQL. Users can write UDFs in Java and add them to Hive for specialized data processing tasks.

HBase Basics

HBase is a NoSQL database built on top of Hadoop's HDFS. It is modeled after Google's Bigtable and is designed to provide real-time read/write access to large datasets.

Concepts in HBase

HBase stores data in tables, but unlike relational databases:

Tables are sparse and column-oriented

Each table has rows, identified by row keys

Data is grouped into column families

Data is stored in versioned cells, based on timestamps

This structure makes HBase suitable for applications needing random access to large-scale data.

Clients in HBase

Clients can interact with HBase using:

Java APIs

Shell commands

REST or Thrift APIs

This allows flexible access from different applications.

Example of HBase Use

Suppose a social media app stores each user's activity logs using row keys as user IDs. With HBase, the app can retrieve and update a specific user's data instantly, even if the system stores millions of records.

HBASE VS. RDBMS

Feature HBase RDBMS

Data Model Column-oriented Row-oriented

Schema Flexible Fixed

Query Language APIs (No SQL) SQL

Access Real-time Real Time Transactional

Best For Big Data with random read/write Structured data with transactions

---

HBASE IS IDEAL WHEN scalability and real-time access are more important than complex querying.

Big SQL

Introduction to Big SQL

Big SQL is IBM's SQL-on-Hadoop engine that allows querying Hadoop data using standard ANSI SQL. It provides full SQL support, including joins, unions, subqueries, and stored procedures.

Big SQL can access data stored in HDFS, Hive tables, HBase, and external databases, allowing integration of structured and unstructured data in a single query environment. It supports high performance, security, and compatibility with enterprise tools.

Big SQL is especially useful for organizations that have skilled SQL developers but want to use Hadoop without learning new languages like Pig Latin or MapReduce.

UNIT V: Data Analytics with R and Machine Learning

DATA ANALYTICS WITH R

R is a powerful programming language specifically designed for statistical computing and data analysis. It provides a wide range of tools for data visualization, statistical modeling, and machine learning. R is open-source, widely supported by a large community, and ideal for analyzing both small and large datasets.

R includes built-in functions and packages like ggplot2, dplyr, and tidyverse that help in cleaning, transforming, visualizing, and interpreting data. Analysts use R for tasks such as trend analysis, hypothesis testing, predictive modeling, and clustering. Its rich set of graphing capabilities makes it easy to create plots, charts, and dashboards for visual insights.

R is also used for Big Data Analytics when integrated with big data tools like Hadoop and Spark, using packages such as rhdfs, rhbase, and sparklyr. These tools allow R to read and process data stored in distributed file systems, making it suitable for enterprise-level analysis.

Machine Learning: Introduction

Machine Learning (ML) is a subset of Artificial Intelligence that enables systems to learn from data and make predictions or decisions without being explicitly programmed. It involves training algorithms using historical data to recognize patterns and improve performance over time.

ML is broadly used in fields like healthcare, finance, marketing, and e-commerce. It powers applications such as spam detection, recommendation systems, credit scoring, and speech recognition. The main idea is to build models that can generalize from known data to unknown situations.

Supervised Learning

Supervised learning involves training a model using labeled data, where each training example is paired with the correct output. The algorithm learns to map input data to desired outputs and is then used to predict results for new data.

Common supervised learning tasks include:

Classification: Predicting a category (e.g., spam or not spam)

Regression: Predicting a continuous value (e.g., house price)

POPULAR SUPERVISED algorithms include:

Linear Regression

Logistic Regression

Decision Trees

Support Vector Machines (SVM)

Random Forests

Neural Networks

THESE MODELS ARE EVALUATED using metrics like accuracy, precision, recall, and mean squared error depending on the task.

Unsupervised Learning

In unsupervised learning, the data is unlabeled, meaning the algorithm tries to find hidden patterns or structures without knowing the output in advance. It is useful for exploring unknown data, grouping similar items, or reducing complexity.

Major tasks in unsupervised learning include:

Clustering: Grouping data based on similarity (e.g., customer segmentation)

Dimensionality Reduction: Reducing the number of variables (e.g., using PCA)

POPULAR UNSUPERVISED algorithms:

K-Means Clustering

Hierarchical Clustering

Principal Component Analysis (PCA)

Autoencoders

UNSUPERVISED LEARNING helps in discovering data patterns, anomalies, and relationships without predefined labels.

Collaborative Filtering

Collaborative Filtering is a key technique used in recommendation systems. It works by analyzing user behavior and preferences to suggest items that a user may like, based on the preferences of other users with similar interests.

Types of collaborative filtering:

User-based filtering: Recommends items based on what similar users liked.

Item-based filtering: Recommends items similar to those the user already liked.

FOR EXAMPLE, IN AN online store, if two users have liked similar books, and one of them buys a new book, the system may recommend that book to the other user. This method is widely used by platforms like Netflix, Amazon, and YouTube.

Collaborative filtering can be implemented using:

Matrix Factorization Techniques (like SVD)

Nearest Neighbor Approaches

Deep Learning Models

Big Data Analytics with Big R

Big R is IBM's tool that integrates R with Big Data technologies like Hadoop and Spark. It enables data scientists to use familiar R syntax while processing large-scale datasets distributed across multiple nodes.

Big R allows:

Running R scripts on Hadoop clusters

Accessing HDFS-stored data directly

Applying machine learning and statistical models on big data

Generating reports and visualizations on large-scale analytics

---

BY COMBINING THE FLEXIBILITY of R with the scalability of Hadoop, Big R bridges the gap between traditional statistics and modern big data environments. It is especially useful for enterprises dealing with terabytes of data and needing advanced analytical capabilities.

About the Author

Nitin Kumar Yadav is a passionate academic contributor, a strategic leader, and a lifelong learner with a vision to make knowledge accessible, relevant, and engaging for the next generation of learners. As a member of the Board of Directors at Sellbrochure IPDP, he brings both leadership and creativity to the field of educational content development and digital publishing.

With a strong belief in the transformative power of technology and data, Nitin has developed a keen interest in areas such as Big Data, Artificial Intelligence, and open-source technologies like Hadoop. His work is driven by the idea that education should be simple, insightful, and deeply connected to real-world applications. This philosophy is clearly reflected in his writing style—where complex topics are explained in a way that students can understand, enjoy, and apply.

Born with an inquisitive mind and a creative soul, Nitin's interests go far beyond academic pursuits. He is deeply passionate about writing, sketching, and music. For him, creativity is not a hobby but a vital part of how he thinks, teaches, and leads. His love for sketching fuels his attention to detail and visualization—qualities that help him explain even the most technical subjects with clarity and imagination.

Nitin is also an enthusiastic online gamer, a hobby that complements his analytical thinking and problem-solving abilities. Gaming, for him, is not just entertainment—it's a dynamic space that fosters strategy, adaptability, and collaboration. These traits have greatly influenced his approach to both leadership and authorship.

At Sellbrochure IPDP, Nitin is known for encouraging original content creation, academic excellence, and digital innovation. He plays a key role in overseeing publication strategies, content quality, and curriculum alignment, ensuring that every book produced under the company banner meets high standards of originality and educational value. His firm commitment to creating original, plagiarism-free educational material has earned him

About the Publisher

About NotesKaro Inc.

Introduction

In the digital age, where education is evolving rapidly and students are striving to keep pace with vast syllabi and competitive pressures, a revolutionary academic platform—NotesKaro Inc.—is emerging as a game-changer. Founded by visionary entrepreneur and author Mrigendra Bharti, NotesKaro Inc. operates under the umbrella of Sellbrochure Vymish Entertainment, a pioneering global publishing initiative.

NotesKaro Inc. is designed with a singular aim: to simplify learning by converting complex lecture notes into concise, concept-rich, and uniquely detailed formats that aid faster and deeper understanding. It empowers students from all academic backgrounds to study smart, perform better, and retain knowledge more effectively.

Whether you're preparing for board exams, college semesters, or competitive tests, NotesKaro Inc. brings academic content to your fingertips—easy to grasp, reliable, and tailored to your syllabus.

A Brainchild of Mrigendra Bharti

NotesKaro Inc. is not just another edtech venture. It is a vision-driven initiative by Mrigendra Bharti, a young entrepreneur, author of over 70 books, and founder of India's fastest-growing free publishing house—Sellbrochure Vymish Entertainment.

Mrigendra started NotesKaro out of a personal realization: students across India often struggle to access organized, well-written notes that are both brief and comprehensive. Most materials available are either too lengthy, overly generic, or riddled with outdated content. NotesKaro was born to solve this very problem.

By creating lecture notes that are concise yet carry deep insight, Mrigendra envisioned a platform where quality meets accessibility—and where learning becomes less burdensome and more efficient.

Part of Sellbrochure – A Publishing Giant

As a proud subsidiary of Sellbrochure Vymish Entertainment, NotesKaro Inc. benefits from an international publishing network spread across 220+ global platforms, including digital libraries, educational marketplaces, and bookstores.

This synergy allows NotesKaro to not only create high-quality academic content but also distribute it worldwide in both print and digital formats, ensuring students everywhere can benefit from it. The brand operates under the same core philosophy as Sellbrochure—education without limitations.

What Makes NotesKaro Inc. Unique?

1. Concise but Not Compromised

Unlike other platforms that provide either over-summarized or overly detailed notes, NotesKaro finds the perfect balance. Each set of notes is carefully structured to ensure:

Crisp explanation of core concepts

Easy-to-remember formats

Bullet points, charts, and illustrations

Chapter-wise clarity with sub-topic divisions

This approach helps students revise quickly and retain information longer.

2. Deep Detailing for Conceptual Clarity

Every topic is treated with the importance it deserves. Even within short notes, NotesKaro adds in-depth insights, examples, and real-world connections to ensure students grasp not just what to learn, but also why and how it matters.

Whether it's technical definitions in engineering, case studies in management, or theoretical concepts in humanities—NotesKaro never compromises on the depth of understanding.

Multi-Format Accessibility

NotesKaro's notes are available in:

PDF format for digital reading

Ebooks for Kindle, Kobo, and other platforms

Print on demand via Sellbrochure's global network

Mobile-optimized formats for easy access on the

Why NotesKaro Inc. Matters Today

In a country with over 300 million students, the need for accessible, affordable, and effective academic resources has never been greater. NotesKaro Inc. stands at the intersection of innovation and necessity.

It represents:

Relief from textbook overload

www.ingramcontent.com/pod-product-compliance
Lightning Source LLC
LaVergne TN
LVHW022028200926
848481LV00007B/2587
* 9 7 9 8 2 3 1 0 3 7 2 4 7 *